better together*

*This book is best read together, grownup and kid.

a kids
book
about

a

kids

book

about

BECOMING a

SIBLING

by Alysa Michelle Tan

A Kids Co.
Editor Emma Wolf
Designer Rick DeLucco
Creative Director Rick DeLucco
Studio Manager Kenya Feldes
Sales Director Melanie Wilkins
Head of Books Jennifer Goldstein
CEO and Founder Jelani Memory

DK
Delhi Technical Team Bimlesh Tiwary Pushpak Tyagi, Rakesh Kumar
Senior Production Editor Jennifer Murray
Senior Production Controller Louise Minihane
Senior Acquisitions Editor Katy Flint
Acquisitions Project Editor Sara Forster
Managing Art Editor Vicky Short
Managing Director, Licensing Mark Searle

First American edition, 2025
Published in the United States by DK Publishing, 1745 Broadway, 20th Floor,
New York, NY 10019

First published in Great Britain in 2025 by
Dorling Kindersley Limited, 20 Vauxhall Bridge Road, London SW1V 2SA
A Penguin Random House Company

The authorised representative in the EEA is
Dorling Kindersley Verlag GmbH. Arnulfstr. 124, 80636 Munich, Germany

A catalog record for this book is available from the Library of Congress.
A CIP catalogue record for this book is available from the British Library.
ISBN: 978-0-2417-4384-3

DK books are available at special discounts when purchased in bulk for sales
promotions, premiums, fund-raising, or education use. For details, contact:
DK Publishing Special Markets, 1745 Broadway, 20th Floor, New York, NY 10019
SpecialSales@dk.com

Printed and bound in China
www.dk.com
akidsco.com

MIX
Paper | Supporting
responsible forestry
FSC™ C018179

This book was made with Forest
Stewardship Council™ certified
paper – one small step in DK's
commitment to a sustainable future.
Learn more at www.dk.com/uk/
information/sustainability

For my Ilias and Zyon. May you never forget that your bond as siblings is one which cannot be broken.

And to Jon, my little brother, who has shown me the true value in having a sibling.

INTRO FOR GROWNUPS

You may be wondering, why write a book about becoming a sibling? It's a common experience, and there are plenty of children's books about it already! But too often, kids' questions and feelings are still left unanswered.

The reality is, becoming a sibling is a big change for a little kid. There are so many emotions and uncertainties, and it can be hard to process such a life-changing event!

I hope this book opens the gates of communication and trust between kids and their grownups. I hope it helps kids better understand what becoming a sibling is all about, welcomes all feelings and questions as valid, and encourages siblings to love their new role and relationship.

HI! MY NAME IS ALYSA. ←

I'm a daughter, a wife, a mother, and I'm also an older sibling.

I became a sibling when I was 2 years old. My brother and I almost shared the exact same birthday!

I remember watching my mom's belly grow.

I remember wanting to spend as much time with her as possible.

And I remember being excited about a new baby joining our family, but nervous about what that change might mean.

My mom was 8 months pregnant
with my brother, Jon, when
my dad passed away.

GROWING UP, IT WAS ALWAYS THE 3 OF US. WE WERE A TEAM.

PLAYING BOARD GAMES
DRESSING UP AND PUTT
WATCHING MOVIES AND
GOING TO AMU
CHEERING EACH OTHER ON
WALKING TO
My brother and I were close and did most things together.
SHARING
CELEBRATING BIRTHDAYS AND
WAKING UP ON CH
AND HONORING OUR
TAKING FAMI

SWIMMING CAMPING
ING ON PERFORMANCES
SHOWS SINGING SONGS
SEMENT PARKS
AT GAMES AND PERFORMANCES
SCHOOL TOGETHER
FAMILY MEALS

Sometimes,
it even felt like
we were twins.

HAVING PARTIES TOGETHER
RISTMAS MORNING
HOLIDAY TRADITIONS
LY VACATIONS

We played together and understood each other and our mom better than anyone else.

Because our dad was gone, I often felt the role and responsibility of helping my mom care for my brother.

Being an older sibling has always felt special and important because I knew the impact I could have on my younger brother.

But the older we got, I realized we had something extra special.

Jon was more than just my brother...

HE WAS MY
BEST FRIEND.

After we graduated high school, we both went far away for college.

But our relationship stayed strong and consistent.

WE MADE IT A PRIORITY TO STAY CONNECTED, NO MATTER WHERE WE WERE.

The times we were back together always felt like no time had passed at all.

And when we both moved back home, we realized just how valuable and powerful our bond is.

Becoming a sibling is a

UNIQUE EX

PERIENCE.

A kid becomes a sibling
when a new kid joins
their family.

And this can happen
many different ways!

SOMETIMES, a baby is born into a family (like my brother).

SOMETIMES, a kid of any age is adopted into a family.

SOMETIMES, a baby is born through surrogacy, which means someone else carries the baby in their womb for your grownup(s).

There are LOTS of ways
to become a sibling.

AND
EACH ONE
IS SPECIAL.

Since becoming a mom of 2, I've been able to witness the bond between my kids change and grow over time.

When I was pregnant with my second baby, I was nervous about how our family dynamic would change.

My oldest had recently turned 2 (just like me when my brother was born), and still needed lots of our time, love, and attention.

(THAT PART NEVER GOES AWAY!)

I wondered about a lot!

How best could we
introduce the 2
of them?

How would our
oldest feel about
sharing his grownups
with someone new?

How would we be able to
meet both of their needs,
without either of them
feeling excluded?

There are lots of questions and feelings that come with growing a family.

AND
THEY ARE ALL
IMPORTANT!

NERVOUS, HAPPY, EXCITED, SAD, ANGRY, ANNOYE
EAGER, JOYOUS, HELPFUL, LONELY, UNEASY, EN
RELIEVED, GUILTY, FRIGHTENED, VULNERAB
GRIEF, ENERGETIC, LOVING, CRUSHED, ANXIO
TENSE, OVERWHELMED, TIRED, ISOLATED, DELIG
ECSTATIC, MISERABLE, PETRIFIED, ENRAG
PANICKED, AGGRAVATED, STUNNED, AMAZE
SHAKEN, SPEECHLESS, UNPREPARED, STARTLED,
ANNOYED, RESTLESS, SCARED, BITTER, CALM,
SHOCKED, ENVIOUS, IRRITABLE, OPPOSED, FEA
VULNERABLE, REJECTED, BRAVE, PROUD, HUNG
ANXIOUS, DEPRESSED, BETRAYED, PEACEFUL, D

Whatever feelings you may ISOLATED, N
have are completely normal. RESTLESS, SC
HELPFUL, LONELY, SHOCKED, ENVIOUS, IRRI
GUILTY, FRIGHTENED, VULNERABLE, REJECTED,
LOVING, CRUSHED, ANXIOUS, DEPRESSED, BETRA
UNEASY, TIRED, ISOLATED, DELIGHTED, GLOOM
MISERABLE, PETRIFIED, ENRAGED, ASTONI
AGGRAVATED, STUNNED, AMAZED, GLEEFUL, OVER
UNPREPARED, STARTLED, WEARY, NERVOUS, HA
SCARED, BITTER, CALM, EXHAUSTED, EAGER,
IRRITABLE, OPPOSED, FEARFUL, SHOCKED, F
REJECTED, BRAVE, PROUD, HUNGRY, SHY, GR
DEPRESSED, BETRAYED, PEACEFUL, DIVIDED, T

, RESTLESS, SCARED, BITTER, CALM, EXHAUSTED,
OUS, IRRITABLE, OPPOSED, FEARFUL, SHOCKED,
E, REJECTED, BRAVE, PROUD, HUNGRY, SHY,
S, DEPRESSED, BETRAYED, PEACEFUL, DIVIDED,
TED, GLOOMY, TERRIFIED, FURIOUS, SURPRISED,
D, ASTONISHED, THRILLED, DISHEARTENED,
GLEEFUL, OVERJOYED, SOMBER, LONESOME,
WEARY, NERVOUS, HAPPY, EXCITED, SAD, ANGRY,
XHAUSTED, EAGER, JOYOUS, HELPFUL, LONELY,
UL, SHOCKED, RELIEVED, GUILTY, FRIGHTENED,
Y, SHY, GRIEF, ENERGETIC, LOVING, CRUSHED,
VIDED, TENSE, OVERWHELMED, UNEASY, TIRED,
RVOUS, HAPPY, EXCITED, SAD, ANGRY, ANNOYED,
RED, BITTER, CALM, EXHAUSTED, EAGER, JOYOUS,
BLE, OPPOSED, FEARFUL, UNEASY, RELIEVED,
RAVE, PROUD, HUNGRY, SHY, GRIEF, ENERGETIC,
ED, PEACEFUL, DIVIDED, TENSE, OVERWHELMED,
, TERRIFIED, FURIOUS, SURPRISED, ECSTATIC,
HED, THRILLED, DISHEARTENED, PANICKED,
OYED, SOMBER, LONESOME, SHAKEN, SPEECHLESS,
PY, EXCITED, SAD, ANGRY, ANNOYED, RESTLESS,
OYOUS, HELPFUL, LONELY, SHOCKED, ENVIOUS,
LIEVED, GUILTY, FRIGHTENED, VULNERABLE,
F, ENERGETIC, LOVING, CRUSHED, ANXIOUS,
SE, OVERWHELMED, UNEASY, TIRED, ISOLATED.

SO, HOW ARE YOU FEELING ABOUT

BECOMING a SIBLING?

Please talk with your grownup, and share what's on your mind. Share it all!

(Or, spend some time thinking on your own, wherever you may be reading.)

Also, use this time to ask questions. What have you been wondering about?

TAKE ALL THE TIME YOU NEED!
I'LL BE HERE WHEN YOU'RE DONE.

No matter how your family is expanding, the reality is things will change.

AND BIG CHANGES ARE HARD FOR EVERYONE!

When change happens,
there are things we can
do to feel more prepared.

ONE OF THE MOST IMPORTANT THINGS IS TO

COMMUNICATE.

Communication helps
all the people in your
family understand
each other better.

Practicing communication helps everyone get on the same page, and the more you do it, the easier it becomes.

You can also read books with your grownups about what's happening, draw or write to express your emotions, and spend quality time together.

ALL ARE GOOD WAYS TO
COPE WITH THE CHANGE.

It's important to remember
that while change is inevitable,
becoming a sibling...

DOESN'T CHANGE THE LOVE YOUR GROWNUPS HAVE FOR YOU.

You may notice that at first, your grownups tend to give a bit more time and attention to the new sibling.

While you are experiencing the change of becoming a sibling, they are adjusting to joining a new family.

AND THAT'S A HUGE
CHANGE, TOO!

Becoming a sibling means your time with your grownups will look different.

Learning to share your grownups can be challenging.

But their devotion to you doesn't
get smaller when someone
new joins your family.

Their love
for you is

EVER-

FLOWING.

**Their hearts simply get bigger
to make room for more people.**

And your role as a sibling is an essential part of helping your new family member feel at home.

YOUR SIBLING RELATIONSHIP
IS SO SPECIAL.

If you choose to, you will have a built-in best friend and a bond to last forever.

And for me,

THAT'S
SOMETHING
I'LL TREASURE
MY WHOLE LIFE.

OUTRO
FOR GROWNUPS

Adjusting to the new reality of being a big sibling can feel overwhelming. Your kid needs support and the reassurance that even though things are going to change, your love will not.

Here are 3 things you can do to help your kid prepare for their new role:

Read books! There are many books that show big siblings in their new role.

Spend quality time. The best way kids communicate is through play. When you set aside a certain amount of time in your day to dedicate undivided attention to each kid, this can help ease the transition, reassure them of your love, and calm their big feelings.

Leave the door open for communication. Check in with your big sibling(s) to ask them how they're feeling and if they have any questions for you.

About The Author

Alysa (Aly) Michelle Tan, M.Ed. (she/her), is an educator, daughter, wife, mother, and an older sibling. She has traveled, taught, and lived abroad, met influential people, and had many life experiences, for which she feels grateful. But above all, she knows her greatest influence is her family.

Aly spends her days raising her 2 little boys, aspiring to teach them many of life's lessons. And one of her favorite lessons is the unique relationship between siblings. Her hope is that this book helps to ease the transition for future big siblings and reminds them of the never-ending love their grownups have for them.

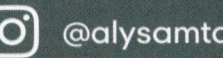 @alysamtan   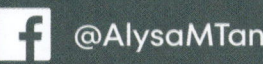 @AlysaMTan

Made to empower.

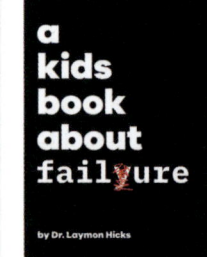 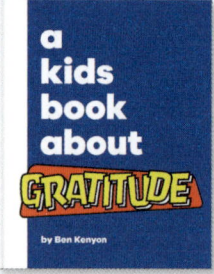   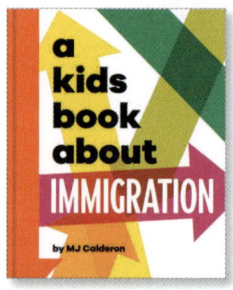

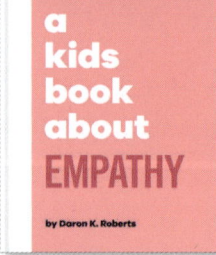 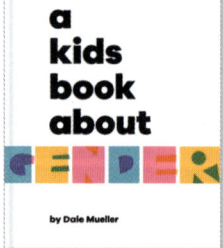 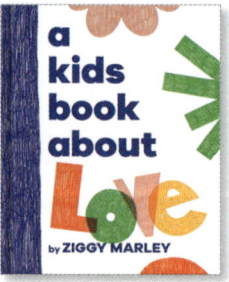 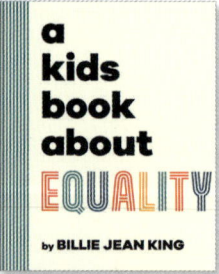 

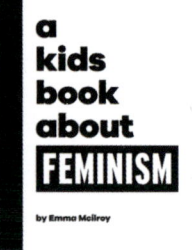  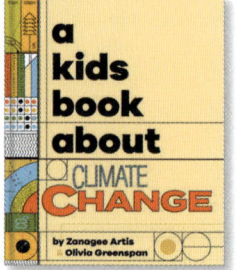  

Discover more at akidsco.com